FITNESS HERO

SLAY YOUR FITNESS DRAGONS AND WIN YOUR FREEDOM

CHRIS ALARCIO

*For the 3Bs, the LBs
and Mom and Dad.*

Disclaimer

The information presented is the author's opinion and does not constitute any health or medical advice. The interpretation of existing creative material is also the opinion of the author and does not reflect the opinions of the original writers and artists. The content of this book is for informational purposes only and is not intended to diagnose, treat, cure, or prevent any condition or disease. Consult a physician before performing any exercise program. It is your responsibility to evaluate your own medical and physical condition, or that of your clients, and to independently determine whether to perform, use or adapt any of the information or content in this book. Any exercise program may result in injury.

CONTENTS

INTRODUCTION

You are about to journey down the path that will lead to the person you're meant to be. Up until this point, you may have been too afraid to find out what that person looks like. Mental resistance has been keeping you from finding that person. But no longer! Now that you've decided to cross the threshold, your journey has become real. You understand that the task isn't just about losing a few pounds—you're taking the journey to become someone else and something else. And that change is terrifying to your ego and the image it has of your self.

Here's the catch: you already have an idea of who this new version of you is. You've caught glimpses in your subconscious without knowing what they meant. You're drawn to that image...but then you quickly reject it because it's too crazy to even imagine. That picture is so far removed from the current version of you that you think there's no way it could happen. No clear path leads from the present-day version of you to the one you keep hidden away from the world. Obviously! After all, if you knew the path and how to travel it, you would have done so already. You haven't taken your first steps because you don't know where to begin. Until now. *Your focus on your health and fitness is your path; the journey is your blueprint.*

What does it mean to be a hero in today's world? Those whom we deem to be heroes tend to put others before themselves, and they also put themselves and their lives on the line for the greater good. Yes, they also mess up a ton and are known to act out of character sometimes when the going gets tough, but the world we know today would not exist without such individuals. It comes with the territory. When we imagine the world as we want it to be, we know we need heroes in all walks of life to make that vision of the future come true.

You're probably asking why we need to talk about heroes in a fitness book. What does being heroic have to do with fitness? If you've picked up this book, I'm guessing you're not looking to be idolized as some kind of heroic figure—you more likely want to learn how to approach your health and fitness with freedom and peace of mind. But remember that "hero" is defined as someone who's admired for courage, outstanding achievements or noble qualities. The noble qualities of the hero are what we're going to focus on. We all have these qualities in some capacity, and you're going to learn to use yours to change yourself and the world around you.

As members of the human race, our most noble quality is arguably our ability to find the best version of ourselves. We become inspirations to others when we live our lives beholden to that image. Finding the best version of ourselves means looking inward; it means discovering what holds us back and how our fears keep us from being our absolute best selves. Only then can we create the kind of change in the world that can and will propel us in our best possible direction.

Our culture today is unfortunately being built by a mishmash of fear-crippled minds making mediocre decisions. We must seek to change this culture! Not by requiring others to change, but by looking inward and finding the hero within.

In the fitness sense, a hero is someone who learns to take ownership of their health and well-being. Our culture and society have evolved greatly over the last few centuries, and so have our medical technologies. While these advancements have led to major breakthroughs, we've also learned to let others take the lead when it comes to our health and well-being. We follow what others do in the hopes that we'll get the same results rather than deciding to do what's best for our individual situations and taking action of our own accord. A lot of the time we're coaxed into exercising and taking better care of ourselves because we think "It's good for me," not because we think "I want to do this."

A hero is someone who realizes that the best version of themself is the healthiest version of themself. A hero chooses to align their life choices to align with that image. They realize that this version is the one that can have the greatest effect on the world around them. Living as this new healthier version, the hero inspires their families, coworkers, friends, partners and so on.

The typical hero's path is a common storyline involving an individual who goes through trials and tribulations and endures a decisive struggle in order to ultimately emerge victorious. Finally, at the end of the journey, the hero comes back home transformed. Such narratives have been told throughout human history, and we continue to see them today in superhero movies, TV shows, books and comics. But the journey also plays out *without* any spandex or cape—as often as the journey takes place on big and small screens, this same journey takes place in real life, too. That's what makes the journey so relatable.

I've been a coach in the fitness industry for over a decade and have encountered many individuals during various stages of their fitness journey. What I've learned is that you can determine someone's stage in the journey by the actions they're taking and the questions they're asking. When people first start out, they ask wide-ranging questions about fitness and nutrition, but as they advance further down the path, they begin to ask questions about how to fine-tune and change their approach. The answers to those more specific questions can differ depending on people's particular goals or life situations. At some point, people become confident enough to take their own approach. They understand how to adjust when they need to, and they know where to find relevant information that will allow them to make further adjustments. The key word there is "adjustments." Keep that in mind as we continue along your own fitness journey.

If you reflect on your own life, I bet you can find an example of having ventured out of your comfort zone, a time when you accomplished a task you never would have thought was possible. And I bet you came out the other side a changed person. Without having known it, as you glimpsed and then reached your new horizon, you experienced the distinct stages of the hero's journey. We'll go over those stages in more detail later, but for now, let's recognize the ability to travel this path and the true power that traversing it holds. If we understand how to create different versions of ourselves, we can understand how to change the world around us, too.

Said another way, in order to change the world, we must first learn what it takes to change ourselves. That's exactly what you'll learn to do through this book and through your fitness journey. Like the journey leading the hero down a path of self-discovery, your fitness journey will take you down a similar path. You'll go from gym newbie to someone who's in complete control of their fitness environment—you'll no longer be the timid gym-goer wondering what you should be doing. And you'll experience freedom by being confident in your fitness approach because you'll know what your goals are and how to continue to tinker away until you achieve them.

Before we get started, though, I have one warning: this book isn't about which exercises are the best or which nutrition plan you should follow. We won't go over body part splits or the proper execution of a power training block. What unites every human who goes through the journey is what they experience in their *minds*. Although every journey is going to look different depending on our individual life circumstances, we experience the same ups and downs, fears, regrets, excitements and inspirations. All things that come from traveling the road less traveled.

Nor is this book about making you a hero for others to worship. This is about making you a hero for *yourself* first. Up until now, you might have been good at showing up for yourself in other parts of your life, but if you picked up this book, chances are you haven't learned to show up for yourself within a health and fitness context, at least not in a way that you feel confident about in a lifelong kind of way. Now, is it possible that you'll become a beacon of health and fitness freedom that other people are inevitably drawn to? Absolutely. Just understand that such attention is a side effect of learning to be a hero for yourself first.

The reason I chose to lay out this book as a map through the hero's path is because we have far too much information available to us today. The meme culture alone has made it very hard to organize all the tips and information we get from the various sources of information available to us. Mind you, a lot of this information is very helpful; memes can be a great way to pass along ideas in simple forms. Many of these sources are great tools we can use to improve ourselves. But the problem is that as a culture, we aren't taught how to digest and use all of this information. We see one quote we like and that's our worldview until we see something else we like. We trap ourselves in endless loops of trying this new fad workout or that headline-hitting diet without making much progress. This book serves as a way to organize all the information we take in and then understand where we are in the process of change.

What you'll read about next is the series of stages most commonly found along someone's fitness journey. You may recognize or see yourself in some or all of these stages; you may have completed a version of this journey in another part of your life. Whatever the case may be, use this book as a guide. Identify where you are on the journey and use the map to anticipate things to come. Part of staying true to the path is knowing how to deal with adversity when it shows up. If you're aware of the challenges that accompany each stage, you'll have a better chance of overcoming those challenges.

This book consists of three parts. Whenever we're trying to learn any new skill or commit to any goal, the general process is the same: first we must learn to show up consistently, then we must learn how to do deep work and focused practice while we're showing up and finally we must learn to integrate what we've learned and disregard what's not working for us (at least, for the time being). Each of these three steps reflects the journey: first the hero must learn their true purpose and begin to show up for that purpose, then they must learn how to be the hero in their story and finally they must learn what it takes to make permanent changes to embody that hero for the rest of their lives.

In Part 1 of the book, you'll learn the characteristics of the everyday world. This world is where you—the hero!—find yourself before you decide to undertake the journey. It's a world where fitness is not among your priorities and anything related to fitness stresses you out. You'll then learn what it means to receive your wake-up call. The call is what inspires you to take a step in the right direction. (You'll also learn why you'll sometimes outright refuse that call.) We'll talk about *what* it means to find a mentor and *how* to find that mentor. These are people (or other resources) who will expand your point of view to inspire you to go all-in on your fitness journey.

In Part 2, you'll learn what it means to begin tinkering and finding out what works for you. We'll touch on the scientific method of thinking and how it will benefit your fitness path. You'll learn rules you can use as guidelines as you run your own self-experiments. You'll learn how your mind and ego will continually seek to derail your consistency and success, and you'll learn how to recognize and overcome those internal roadblocks so that you can experience freedom in your health and fitness.

In Part 3, you'll find out how to solidify your mindset, thus enabling you to keep yourself on track through almost any situation. You'll learn that something will always be trying to pull you away from your discipline, consistency and freedom, and you'll learn what it means (and takes) to change your mindset. You'll go from expecting those roadblocks to stop one day to expecting them to be there for the rest of your life. But that's fine, because you'll learn how to navigate past those blocks. Then you'll learn how to use your newfound growth mindset to keep yourself from stagnating. By the end of the book, you'll have a roadmap you can use to figure out how to deal with any problem you may come across.

Now that you know what's in store for you on the road ahead, it's time to suit up! Don your cape and cowl, your vibranium suit or just your best workout attire. In the words of a certain caped and dark-winged crusader, "Let's get dangerous."

PART 1
SHOW UP

CHAPTER 1

THE EVERYDAY WORLD, THE WAKE-UP CALL & IGNORING THE CALL

———————◆———————

One of the most common characteristics of a hero is that they show up when they're needed the most. Author Joseph Campbell wrote, "We're not on our journey to save the world but to save ourselves. But in doing that, you save the world." One of the hardest parts for the hero is that they don't always know how to *be* a hero or why they're needed to show up. At least, not at first. It's not until they realize they must show up for *their own selves first* that they can have the positive impact on the world they envision having.

Our personal fitness is much the same. We start out by doing the things we think we're supposed to do to fit some image of "fitness." It isn't until we start to really focus on what works best for us and what we need in a health and wellness sense that we start to own our fitness. This ownership of our health is what leads to a feeling of freedom and deepens our ability to have a positive effect on the world around us.

Campbell is well known for laying out the steps of the hero's journey; later on, Christopher Vogler created his version of the journey as well. The journey describes how a hero goes through their transformation and accomplishes something great, sometimes for the world and sometimes just for themselves. Your fitness journey is much the same— you too will seek to transform yourself in ways that are not necessarily clear at the beginning of your journey. We'll be looking at 9 possible stages for your own journey through the fitness realm. You may recognize some of these stages, but you may not have yet ventured far enough to have experienced others.

In terms of the information you'll come across along your journey, the fitness world is rapidly expanding— new information and rebranded knowledge is churned out daily. The firehose effect of the internet can make it nearly impossible to actually *use* any of this knowledge. With too many choices and so many different voices and opinions, it's hard to know which direction to take.

Enter this book! Use it as a guide whether you're somewhere in the middle of your fitness journey or you're just starting out. In the coming pages, you'll find your next steps and you'll understand where you'll encounter pitfalls. You'll learn ideas and concepts to help avoid those pitfalls, including ideas about how to escape from them should you find yourself stuck. Eventually, you'll end up using this book as a reference to aid in your journeys *outside* of the fitness realm, too.

The Everyday World

Imagine living a life with no surprises—you know what to expect at every twist and turn, and it feels like you're just going through the motions of living life with nothing really exciting to look forward to.

Every journey starts in the same place: the everyday world. This is where we find the status quo, where nothing is out of place and everything seems mundane. It's the same house and the same boring rooms you always visited before you entered the portal to another world at the back of the wardrobe. It's the Shire in all its familiarity before you got called to a grand adventure. It's Harry Potter's world, a place where nobody wanted him, a place where he woke up every morning in the cupboard under the stairs and had to wear his cousin's hand-me-down clothes. It's Rose before she meets Jack on the grandest of all ships.

Regardless of where you start, you'll be feeling the same way: uninspired. You're unaware of any challenges ahead. You don't know how hard it is to maintain consistent training, and you're unaware of what discipline can do for your life both inside and outside of the gym. You may conceptually understand that exercise is good for you, but because you've never really felt how it could benefit you, the idea of the benefits of exercise aren't tangible to you. They aren't *real*.

The only way to make those benefits real and therefore persuasive is to get out of the everyday world and focus on your fitness and *take action*. This isn't to say that having ideas and theories about exercise is wrong—ideas are a great place to start. But actually creating change in your life means those ideas must turn into actions at some point. And you must put your actions into the physical world by deciding to carry them out. It is truly that simple. However, the process that leads to that decision doesn't always follow a straight line, nor is the process itself always easy.

Growing up, I was transported out of my everyday fitness world through sports. I would watch college and professional athletes on TV and marvel at their skill and poise. In contrast, when I first started playing sports, I was unsure of myself and lacked skill. I was nothing at all like the athletes I saw on TV! It wasn't until I learned how to practice that I began to see a difference. Focus, discipline and thousands of repetitions put me on the path to improvement.

It was a lesson I took with me when I started to do strength training in high school. And it's what led me to the coaching path when I understood that deep practice was a lesson that other people needed help to learn.

For some of us, deciding to engage in consistent exercise has become almost automatic. For others, exercise seems like more of a chore and a hassle and working out feels much less like an opportunity to improve their life. Maybe you're in the latter camp. Sure, you know you're supposed to do it, but knowing that something is good for you and deciding to take action are two different things. We know that we should do a lot of things for ourselves, yet we often don't end up doing them. We don't take action out of fear or because we don't want to make too many waves. We don't take action a lot of the time because we're comfortable staying right where we are.

It's that very feeling of comfort that keeps you from removing yourself from the everyday world. You're *comfortable* not taking complete ownership of your health and wellness. You're *comfortable* leaving all of your decisions up to others when it comes to the health of your own body. People often wait until something is wrong—sometimes *really* wrong— before they start trying to improve their health. With the miracles of modern medicine, you can wait until something breaks down to take action, and most of the time, you will indeed still be okay in the end.

The problem is that waiting until you get bad news means you're only *re*acting to problems. Taking ownership of your health and fitness means you're *pro*actively taking steps to prevent those issues from happening or at least get out ahead of them. Say you know your family has a history of heart disease. Taking ownership means making exercise a priority before your doctor tells you to.

However, the concept of proactive action is a lot easier said than done. We get trained from an early age to react and not take proactive steps, especially when it comes to our health. We assume that if nothing hurts and we're not sick, we're okay and nothing needs to improve. We are never taught the fact that even if nothing seems wrong, there's always room for improvement. There's always room to improve our understanding of our body and mind. Our health involves so many variables! We can always try to chip away at and improve on something. An individual who's proactive is always thinking about the next thing they can work on.

Of course, at this stage of the journey, none of these ideas are likely to be a solid part of your thought process yet. So what gets the ball rolling?

The Wake-Up Call

> *Picture this: it's been a while since you noticed something off about the world, but you don't know quite yet how to go about fixing it. Then one day, you're privy to a new piece of information or you earn a newfound ability or power. You suddenly see a way to begin fixing all the things around you that you couldn't fix before.*

The next phase on the hero's journey is called "the call to action." In this phase, the hero steps away slightly from their comfort zone as they catch a glimpse of something outside of their normal, everyday surroundings. Once the hero sees whatever that is, their path to adventure (and their resulting journey) becomes clear. It's the moment when the hero realizes that no one else wants to take the ring to rule all rings back to fires that forged it, so they must find their own inner strength to do so.

While your own wake-up call may not look as cool as a scene in a Peter Jackson movie, the call can truly be a life-or-death issue. I've encountered many clients whose doctors suggested that they exercise or risk a significant decline in their health. But being informed that you have a health issue isn't always the wake-up call—you may do what you're supposed to do or you may not. The *real* call comes when you realize that *yes,* you *are* capable of changing your life through fitness and exercise.

If you've never embraced this truth, it can be mind-blowing to find out that you can indeed lose a few pounds. You then realize that if you focus your attention on a goal for a few months, you can improve your health. You may even put on some solid muscle mass while you're at it. When you make changes like that, you catch a glimpse of what wasn't possible in your everyday world. And the moment when you understand that *you have the power to change* is when the adventure truly begins.

In *Iron Man*, Tony Stark gets captured by a group of terrorists. He manages to build a robotic suit and set himself free. Tony then builds an updated design of his suit when he returns home. But even after having done all that, his wake-up call doesn't come until he discovers his company sold weapons to the very terrorists who captured him. That's when Tony takes it upon himself to change the situation and begins using the Iron Man suit to do good in the world.

Letting the Call Go to Voicemail

Remember that call you just received? The one that gave you permission to start making changes to the world around you? Yeah, you looked into it...and it turns out that all the stuff you dreamed about doing is going to be way harder than you thought. So hard, in fact, that you're hoping you can put your volunteering hand back down so you can say "Pass!" instead.

Leaving the everyday world isn't always simple, and responding to the wake-up call is no walk in the park, either. It might seem like once somebody feels how effectively they can make changes, they'd just be able to make those changes all of the time...except the truth is that making changes and getting out of our comfort zone is hard. Really hard. Leaving our comfort zone goes against our natural tendencies, and we get uncomfortable because our minds prioritize self-preservation and safety.

Our nervous system consists of a brain, a spinal cord and nerves that extend to all parts of our bodies. This system runs our bodies and gives us information about the world around us; we base many of our decisions on that information. Say our nose picks up a peculiar scent that smells rotten. Our nervous system tells us not to eat the bowl of rice we've left out for two weeks. Or perhaps we're walking through the jungle and our eyes see the brush moving. Our brain tells us to pause and assess the situation to see if it's the wind or a giant jungle cat.

Our nervous system's underlying mechanisms attempt to keep us safe. Familiar and repeatable signals, for example, register as being "safe." But here's the catch: even things that are bad for us can feel safe simply because they feel familiar and predictable. *Un*predictable situations can involve variables that we don't understand and that can therefore make us feel unsafe. So when we receive a call to adventure and start to view the world differently, our nervous system can interpret those differences as being unpredictable. And therefore unsafe and undesirable.

One thing to note is that we don't only deal with our nervous system when it comes to making changes— we must also deal with the limits of what we're willing to put up with. When we take different actions and make changes, those actions must continue in order for the changes to be permanent. Making some changes in our lifestyle in the short term is doable, we find, but having to consider making those changes for the rest of our life can be a daunting task…and one that many people reject outright.

Even when you're the hero in your own story, another reason why you might refuse the call is that you're afraid of failure. There's an inherent risk to your ego when you take different actions in an attempt to get different results—those actions may not yield the results you want. The risk to your ego is that you may look dumb for trying something different and failing.

Think about this: even Luke Skywalker didn't want to leave his home despite yearning for adventure. When presented with the opportunity, he immediately shrank back into his everyday world. It wasn't until stormtroopers killed his aunt and uncle that he finally agreed to leave with Old Ben.

From a fitness standpoint, the journey usually goes something like this: you decide on a new fitness goal and start going to the gym. After a few days, you realize that things aren't going to happen overnight—you'll have to keep making the effort to go to the gym week in and week out. You know you're going to have to deal with all the pains and hassles of getting there. And you know you're going to have to deal with all the weirdness and all of your anxieties once you *are* there. After a while, you think "I don't want to look dumb out here" or "This isn't worth it." And then you stop going altogether.

Don't get discouraged if this has been your experience thus far. When I worked in a commercial gym, I learned that people would buy a membership and never set foot in the gym once! And these people paid their memberships for months or years without ever actually going to the gym! So if you're hesitant after receiving your call, don't worry—that's actually right where you should be.

Which brings us to how you can circumvent refusing the call. When you refuse the call to adventure, what you're saying is "I don't think I can do this" or "I don't deserve this" or "This isn't for me." One way to free yourself from these kinds of thought patterns is to change your point of view with the help of a mentor. A mentor is a person or piece of knowledge that can remove your mind from its current box. In a nutshell, learning from mentors allows you to experience freedom from your everyday world. Which is why we're going to talk about that part of your journey next.

CHAPTER 2

FINDING A MENTOR
AND GEARING UP FOR
THE ROAD AHEAD

Mentors

You must first accept your role on your journey before the mentor appears. Only then will the universe know to send help.

The next phase of the hero's journey is when the hero gets a push from someone or something. This push usually comes along right when the hero needs it. At that point, the hero may feel ready to embrace the challenge and go full speed ahead...but the hero also doesn't know what they don't know.

They need someone to provide them with the tools or mentor(s) they'll need to navigate their new environment.

Mentors can come in many forms: wise old wizards, maintenance workers with mad martial arts skills, street-racing legends. Mentors can even come in the form of an object, like a book that provides a blueprint to success or a map that shows the hero where the treasure is.

On your own fitness journey, you may encounter many such mentors in the form of coaches. They can be a coach you hire or whose work you read online or whose presentations and videos you watch. Coaches can be a friend or an acquaintance who's gone through the same type of transformation as what you're going through. Whatever the case, the mentor must give you insights into the direction you're intending to go—in short, the mentor must give you an "aha!" moment. That moment happens when you see an idea you hadn't considered before or hadn't understood how you could apply to your own situation. This type of realization alters the way you approach your journey and sets you on a path you weren't previously aware of. At the very least, it sets you on a path you weren't able to find on your own.

Don't underestimate the power of the "aha!" moment. Many sources of information will tell you things you may already know and are valuable precisely because of that—they confirm your intuition and give you confidence to try things out. But also know that the reason you'll likely get stuck at some point along your journey is because you'll come to a point where you won't know how to proceed. You may need a few tips on how to improve your performance, or you may not know why you aren't getting the results you think you should be getting. That's when the mentor can provide you with a point of view you hadn't considered or didn't know existed. And that moment of insight provides freedom from the anxiety of not knowing the next step.

In the movie *Major League*, flame-throwing pitcher Rick Vaughn was about to get demoted to the minor leagues. Why? Despite throwing extremely hard, Vaughn couldn't throw strikes. But then his manager Lou Brown noticed that Rick had trouble seeing a poster that was just a few feet away and realized that Vaughn's problem wasn't a mechanical problem related to his pitching technique—Vaughn's problem was that he *literally couldn't see* the strike zone. Vaughn got a pair of glasses and was off to the races. Of course, in a real baseball organization, Vaughn would have had a physical exam and they would have caught his vision problems. But I digress. The point is that it often takes someone outside of ourselves to provide the insight that gets us to the next step on our path.

Your mentor will give you the general lay of the land—as Musafa said, "Everything the light touches is your kingdom." Your mentor will give you the dos and don'ts and what to look out for and which people to trust and so on. On your fitness journey, your mentor will provide you with the kind of tips and support that align with your goals. But your mentor should also prepare you to eventually *not* rely on them. They understand that they have a limited ability to lead you down the path— eventually, you must learn to walk on your own.

So how do you find such a mentor and what do you look for?

Looking for a mentor on your fitness journey means finding sources of information that provide insights into your goals. If you want to learn how to perform a squat better, you might not want to hire a running coach first. That isn't to say that a running coach wouldn't know how to teach a squat, but it may not be their first priority/core area of expertise in their capacity as a trainer. You want to learn from people who are experts at whatever you're trying to do. However, experts in adjacent fields may have some important details to share as well. Remember that the goal of finding a mentor is to provide you with the knowledge you need to get out of your comfort zone and help you take the next step.

Your mentor should have knowledge of the roadblocks you're going to face and have at least an idea of how you can get around them. However, do *not* expect your mentor to do the work for you! As the saying goes, you can lead a horse to water but you cannot make it drink. Your mentor should do the same for you. Take this book, for example. I wrote it with the intention of leading you to water via the map that takes you through the journey. I *know* that path. What I *don't* know is anything about you as an individual. While I can make suggestions and give my opinion about how you should approach this journey, I cannot make any decisions for you and I cannot take any actions for you. The mentor provides insight and feedback, but the decisions and actions are made by and taken by *you*. That's how the role of the mentor works.

In addition, the mentor must be okay with you surpassing them in some ways. Obi Wan knew he wasn't supposed to be the one to defeat Darth Vader even though (spoiler alert!) he was Vader's mentor at one point. He knew that defeating Vader was Luke's job. So Obi Wan did everything in his power to prepare Luke for the task, as did Yoda. The same goes for me as the author of this book: I want you to take the ideas I've given you and exceed any expectations I may have had for you. My ideas are limited by my mind and my imagination. In some ways, *your* ideas about how to implement my advice are going to be different than what *I* think can be done. It's up to you to take my advice and make something more of it. What direction you'll decide to take is a mystery to me, but I do wish with all my heart that you'll go further than I've dreamed possible.

But back to finding a mentor. The last aspect you want to consider is availability. Initially, you'll want to find the most well-respected and well-known person you can. It makes perfect sense to learn from someone who's at the top of their field. After all, there's a reason why people say "To be the best, you must learn from the best." However, there's a caveat: people at the top of their fields often have high demands on their time and attention. That's not to say you aren't deserving of help from someone very successful, but they also have the right to use their time as they see fit. And frankly, they'll rarely spend their limited time on helping someone who's just starting out on their journey, at least not in a one-on-one setting. So start by finding someone who's a few steps ahead of where you're at now. Chances are they'll have a bit more time for you if they're not yet at the very top of their field.

But! There's a workaround to the problem of top-tier mentors not being readily available: you can get into their mindset through the magic of the internet, where it's easy to access anyone's thoughts and ideas without taking up any of their time. Podcasts, webinars, online courses and plain old books are ways to soak up ideas and mindsets without the creator of those thoughts having to be in the same room with you. This works particularly well for people who like to figure out their own way of doing things. You can take all of the guidelines those mentors give and use them to come to your own conclusions. And if you're still not sure what actions to take, in-person mentors can serve as guides, too—they can observe your specific situation and make recommendations.

Gearing Up

> *The road to fitness is one we travel our whole lives. Success on this path means accepting, right now, that it is a lifelong commitment.*

Once you find a mentor, you're going to want to make sure you have the right tools to go all-in on your fitness journey. This is the scene in the movies where the hero gathers up their gear before facing the long hard road ahead—they're packing up all the items they anticipate they'll need to deal with the challenges they may face, and they may even have a mentor who provides them with gadgets or weapons to deal with those challenges.

You'll do the same thing at this stage of your own fitness journey, except it's not about packing up your gym bag with pre-workout, lifting straps and chalk. As you depart from your everyday world, the gearing up you are going to do happens in your *mind*. Remember that the fitness journey is both physical and mental. To reach your physical goals, you must first change the way you view the world and what you believe is possible within it.

You're going to want to adopt what author Carol Dweck calls a "growth mindset." Someone with a growth mindset believes that all things in life are skills that can be fine-tuned and improved upon. Personal growth is at the heart of any journey, but even so, the hero often starts out with the opposite of a growth mindset, which is a "fixed mindset." Someone with that mindset believes we're either born with talent or we're not and there's nothing we can do about it. A person with a fixed mindset says, "I'm just not good at this particular thing," whereas someone with a growth mindset says, "I can get better at this particular thing if I focus my time and attention on it."

Often, the mentor is the person who shows you how much you can grow, but how well you're able to execute the process of growing depends on whether you have a growth mindset or a fixed mindset. In other words, does the way you approach challenges make you reach further than you'd thought you could, or you do feel like just giving up?

To move from one step to the next on any journey requires growth and improvement. Think about any mentor you've had in your professional or academic life. They probably presented you with a challenge that required you to do more than you'd thought you could. Your fitness mentor should do the same in some way, shape or form—they must add a growth mindset to how you view the world. Otherwise, you'll lack the most important tool you need to get past your roadblocks.

The next conversation you'll want to have is with yourself—you need to honestly assess what you're willing to do to reach your goal. Over the years, many people have told me that they want to train a certain amount of times per week, often setting a high bar like 5 or 6 times a week. But they don't say this because they actually *want* to work out 5 to 6 times a week—they just assume more is better in this context. (It's true that more *can* be better if you're actually willing to *do* more.) Really, these well-intentioned people may only want to train twice a week. And they'll keep beating themselves up for not doing the "required" 6 days a week that they saw someone else doing.

Full disclosure: only training twice a week may not be enough for you to reach your goal. If that's honestly the most time you're willing to give, you may have to change your goals and expectations. But that doesn't mean you can't try to get maximum results while only training 2 days a week! You just have to realize that the results are probably going to look different than what it would look like if you *were* willing to train 6 days a week.

Whatever the determined amount of effort you wish to put in may be, you must *maintain your efforts*. Consistent, focused practice is the key to attaining any goal. You must understand the differences between being all-in and still having one foot in your everyday world. Deciding to go all in is what author Steven Pressfield calls "turning pro."

Pressfield writes about an invisible force that keeps us from doing the things we know we need to do. He names this force the "Resistance." It's the invisible wall we hit when we have a deadline looming. It's the force that'll make us do anything other than work on our project. It can come up in the form of watching another hour of TV instead of going to the gym, or it can keep us from writing the book we promised ourselves we were going to write by making us get obsessed with being a famous social media influencer instead. (That might have been a bit too personal, but you get the point.)

Turning pro means deciding to tackle the work you know you have to do head-on. No more side quests derailed by the Resistance! No more "I'll get to this when I have time"! When you decide to go all in by turning pro, your life will look different. You're giving up your life of comfort—a.k.a. your everyday world—to venture out and become what and who you were always meant to be. In terms of your health and fitness, you'll become someone who has complete ownership over the process of keeping themself healthy and fit. You'll no longer defer to what others might think. You'll know what's best for you and you'll stick to it without distracting yourself with fad diets or trendy programs. Doesn't sound so hard, right? You just do what you find works best for you.

Except it's very hard to look Resistance in the eye and still do what needs doing. You'll find every possible reason to *not* to get off your butt because it's easier to stay exactly where you are than it is to make changes. As we've discussed, making changes takes you out of your comfort zone. Not only that, it takes a lot of courage to face discomfort day in and day out. But discomfort is a requirement! You must have the courage to walk towards discomfort. Such courage is earned by deciding to turn pro.

You *must* grasp the concept of turning pro before you take the next step. You *must* be willing to leave your comfortable life behind. You *must* be willing to be confused, lost and on the verge of quitting in order to put yourself in a position where you can finally find your own way. Finding your way can be tough—it takes deep thought, considerable self-reflection and a whole lot of courage to travel the road less traveled. And it's harder to know if you're doing the right thing because there are fewer signs to validate your path. You *must* be able to trust your own efforts and your own ideas. This is what it means to turn pro.

Once you *have* taken hold of the idea of turning pro, you're ready to cross the threshold into the unfamiliar world, the world where the real adventure begins. Up to this point, you've only dabbled with adventure because you've kept a lifeline to your old life and your old comforts—you know, the ones you're used to.

The *real* journey begins when you enter your new world with a new mindset. You have decided that this version of yourself is who you are now. And you will fight to maintain this You 2.0 throughout all the trials you're about to go through.

CHAPTER 3

LEARNING TO SHOW UP

———◆———

The deceptive thing about the red pill/ blue pill choice is that it's not just one decision. Sure, it's your initial move in a different direction, but it's also literally every decision you'll make after that. Does your current choice move you along your chosen rabbit hole or does it move you in the opposite direction?

When you learn what it means to show up for the fight is when the journey starts to take off. As the hero enters the new and unfamiliar world, there's no turning back—they'll either make it to the end of the journey or die trying. They'll conquer the dragon and find the hidden treasure...or they'll experience one too many missteps along the way and the dragon will catch them slipping. Of course, there's no actual dragon on your fitness journey, only a dragon in the form of Pressfield's Resistance. But showing up *does* symbolize your commitment to battle Resistance on a daily basis. You must accept that an invisible force will always try to keep you from getting your work done. It will not stop! Which is why you can't, either.

Up until now, you've experienced some genuine starts and some false starts. You've found ways to shift your mindset and you've made the commitment to yourself to go all in on your fitness. But another thing you must shift when you're entering this phase of your journey is your expectations. You might be thinking you've conquered your fears once and for all; maybe you understand your anxieties on a deeper level. Even if you do, however, that doesn't mean they'll disappear forever! Think of it like a light dimmer switch: the more mindful you are of your fears, the easier it will be to lower the intensity of those emotions.

When you can let intense feelings pass without taking brash action, you can maintain control over your actions. That's crucial, because although you cannot make your emotions disappear, you *can* keep them from influencing the actions you take. You'll even start to recognize that some of your actions are direct reactions to your fears and anxieties. Over time, you'll be able to recognize your innate desire to act on those feelings of fear and you'll be able to keep yourself from doing so. That means you'll begin to take actions that keep you on your path rather than being driven by your fear. Familiarizing yourself with your fears and anxieties means you'll be in better control of your actions. That's when you'll begin to make better decisions...and *that's* how you'll begin to slay your inner dragons.

Another way to look at the idea of showing up is a concept called "burning your ships." This relates to the era when explorers would find a piece of land and catalog it before returning to their place of origin to report what they had found. Sometimes, if the goal was to settle the new land, the explorers would burn their ships once they got there. Figuratively and literally, then there was no way back. The explorers solidified their goal by cutting off access to their former lives.

On your fitness journey, "burning your ships" is the act of deciding to leave your non-fitness-focused world behind. You're saying to yourself, "I am going to figure out this path or die trying." While that may sound extreme, it's the attitude you *must* take in order to really get to where you want to go.

To clarify, I don't mean you're going to push your efforts past the absolute limit of your body's capabilities. That's not a healthy idea in most cases. What I'm saying is that you're going to decide to tackle your new fitness path head–on! Your responsibility is to always do your best to stick to your new path no matter what. Doing so may mean dying along the way for any reason, predictable or not, fair or not. You need to consistently ask yourself, "If I were to die in this instant, would I be at peace knowing I've done my best to stick to my path?"

For many of us, the answer to this question is a resounding "No!" We fear the concept of death, and rightly so. We all want to do certain things in our lives before we die. We don't know what will happen when we die. We worry we won't get everything done that we've promised ourselves we'll do before we die.

But the noble path of the hero isn't centered around the ultimate achievement, whatever that may be— the noble goal of the hero is to always stick to the path regardless of any and all external and internal forces. Think of heroes who make a vow to never kill their enemies. They make that vow despite the atrocities their enemies commit. In those stories, some people always insist that killing is the only way to resolution, forcing the hero to decide which path they want to take: the one they feel is right or the one everyone else tells them to take.

To mirror this choice on your fitness journey, you must reframe your future goals and center them around your fitness and health and not just around career achievements. If you do—if you *consistently* work on your health—you're putting yourself in a position to do great things in the future. The most fit version of yourself will have the energy and longevity to achieve your future goals.

That said, you shouldn't avoid working on your future goals while you work on your health. The two are not mutually exclusive. In fact, if you prioritize your health, you'll keep the paths to all of your other goals open! You'll have the energy to work both your day job *and* your side gig. You'll have the energy to raise children *and* build a business empire. Let's face it— most goals are significantly harder to reach if you're in poor health. Thus, your future goals depend on you doing your best to stick to your path in the moment or die trying.

The last thing you'll want to address before you make the leap into your new world is making sure the stakes feel higher. If everything feels the same, you're probably not taking much of a chance. But you're not playing pickup basketball anymore! You're stepping into the *real* arena, whether you realize it or not. That's what it means to turn pro and cross the threshold. You must act as if you're getting paid to play the game you're about to play, and that game is your fitness journey. You're going to attack this journey with the same intensity as a professional athlete would, except you're going to do it while no one is watching. That's what makes the act truly heroic.

Since the stakes are higher when you prioritize your fitness, expect some turbulence—if you experience smooth sailing, then you probably haven't left your everyday world behind yet. Also, before you begin your journey, you must prepare to encounter roadblocks. Know that you cannot accurately predict what these future roadblocks will be. Not all of them, at least.

You *can* prepare for some hang-ups if you're honest with yourself about the way your mind works. If you know you aren't willing to go to certain lengths to achieve a gym goal, you're going to have to figure out another way. The goals of the rest of this book are to give you insights into looking for your looming roadblocks and to teach you how to reframe your thoughts to find new ways around them.

To become a master at maneuvering around such problems, you must first learn how to master yourself. That means seeking to understand yourself. You have to know *why* you want to do what you want to do in life, and you must also understand your purpose. Are you working out more so you can remain healthy and provide for your family? Are you hitting the gym 6 days a week because you want to look better so you can boost your confidence? Are you building your confidence so you can use it to achieve success in other parts of your life? There are no wrong answers. You just need to ask yourself if your reason is still good enough for you. If it is, keep going. If it's not, step back and reassess. Keep asking yourself "Why?" until you get down to the nitty-gritty details.

If any part of your why has to do with what someone *else* thinks you should be doing, be wary, because if that's the case, then at some point the process will become about pleasing someone else. That can lead to resentment because you'll start to neglect what you really want in life. You must shift your focus to make sure you're doing what you're doing first and foremost for yourself. That may seem a bit selfish, and to some degree it is. But if you're going to help anyone else, you must be at your best. You cannot serve others by showing up in life with just a fraction of your full potential. At least, not in the heroic way you're thinking of and want to do.

Now that you have some cornerstone tools like having a growth mindset and your why, you're ready to proceed. The next step in the process is going to be the most time-consuming one you'll encounter in your journey, because it's time to step out of your everyday world and into the actual arena. You're going to spend a good amount of time learning about health and fitness! And you're going to get your hands dirty.

Reflections for Part 1 of Your Fitness Journey

➢ Begin to write your fitness story. You can do this manually or in your mind:

➢ Ask yourself what your everyday world is/was like when it comes to fitness.

➢ Try to remember what your fitness call to action looked and felt like.

➢ Are you currently refusing that call? If so, why? If not, how did you get past your refusal?

➢ Who are some possible mentors? What information and educational materials are available to you?

➢ How does Resistance show up in your journey?

➢ Do you posses a growth or fixed mindset? How can you tell?

➢ What can Turing Pro look like on your journey? How will you burn your ships?

PART 2

DEEP WORK IN THE TRENCHES

CHAPTER 4

GETTING YOUR UNOFFICIAL DEGREE IN FITNESS

---◆---

> *The reality is that we aren't taught how to use our bodies at a young age. There's no user's manual for us to follow. We are more or less left to our own devices when it comes to understanding how our bodies work. Thus we spend our adult years getting an unofficial degree in using our bodies.*

As a new coach in the industry in the late 2000s, one of my biggest sources of information was the internet. At the time, the online space wasn't the social media free-for-all it is today—most of the articles I read and the websites I visited were written by professional coaches who had long, successful histories of training clients around the world. Many of these coaches had advanced academic degrees that I didn't possess. Still, they never pointed at the letters after their names as a reason why their advice should hold water. According to many of these coaches, the time they had spent "in the trenches" was what made them credible.

To these coaches, anyone could get certifications or degrees. While it took hard work to get those credentials, they weren't what made coaches great. The thing that made coaches great was the time they had spent actually *coaching* people. That's where they learned what worked with people in the real world—they got to see firsthand whether or not the theories in books applied to every situation. (They didn't.)

Back when I first started coaching, in the trenches was where I tested out what I knew by explaining concepts to people who had no background in fitness. A simple test of this for me was when I realized that certain cues for certain exercises didn't work for everyone. The main cue for a client's hips when teaching them to squat, for example, was to tell them to "sit back like they were sitting on a chair." While that worked for some clients, it didn't for others. I saw that if I wanted to teach a squat, I was going to have to find several different ways of explaining it. The only way to learn what worked was to experiment: to work on the gym floor directly with clients. In the trenches. That was a big part of my journey as a coach.

To relate that experience to our journey, as the hero crosses into their new world, they have to learn how to navigate their new surroundings. This phase usually takes the longest because the hero faces many tests. These trials are necessary to make sure the hero is ready to go the distance. The test phase is where the hero uses their new mindset to face new challenges. They no longer run from every hard and unfamiliar challenge—they've learned to stay in an uncomfortable state and find out what they're made of. The hero learns who they are even while fighting whatever the villain throws at them.

On your fitness journey, this phase is when you start figuring out what *actually* works for you as opposed to continuing to do what you *think* you're supposed to be doing. Make no mistake: if you want to own your health and fitness, this is a step you must take. There is simply no way around the hands-on learning you get from showing up day in and day out and doing the work. There is no shortcut. You can get away with relying on a coach or trainer to give you a plan, yes, but you must simultaneously learn as much as you can from your coach. Increasing your knowledge base will make it easier to own your process when you're ready to do so. Think of this phase as one big science experiment.

In science experiments, the variable N represents the amount of test cases. Not surprisingly, when publishing studies for peer review, experimenters want to have a large N group. This accounts for different types of people and different types of reactions to the experiment. Having a large N group can give the reader of the study confidence in the conclusions that were drawn from the experiment.

However, you aren't going to be conducting a large-N experiment in this phase—you'll be conducting experiments where N always has a value of 1. These are self-experiments, and *you* are the sole test subject. You're going to try different strategies when it comes to health, exercise and nutrition. You're going to learn why things work for you and under which circumstances they work best. Remember that the process of finding out what works and what doesn't is an ongoing one. Adjusting methods to better suit your life and personality gives you ownership over your well-being.

Chances are you already use this process in other aspects of your life: you switch between different shampoos to see which one creates the effect you want, for example, and you test different routes to your new job to see which one works best for your commute. Testing different methods against each other and carefully tracking the results is called "the scientific method." It's a way of verifying the claims of scientific inquiries.

Say you want to know how to make the best webs for swinging through the streets of Queens. In that case, you would first have to establish a hypothesis—maybe a particular combination of X, Y and Z chemicals in specific ratios would make the best web materials for what you need. Then you'd test your hypothesis. You'd make a batch of that exact mixture along with several other mixtures using different ratios and different chemicals. You would observe each mixture while the hero swings along and fights crime. You could then draw conclusions to answer your original question and propose any necessary follow-up questions. Perhaps one of the other mixtures—one you hadn't initially thought of—worked better than the original X, Y and Z chemicals.

Now let's take that kind of scientific method thinking and apply it to trying an elimination diet:

- Ask a question: "Are there any specific foods/food groups that may be derailing my progress?" An elimination diet requires you to avoid eating a food/food group that might be detrimental to your health.
- Establish a hypothesis: The variables in this scenario are different foods/food groups. You can hypothesize that Food/Food Group X is making you feel terrible.
- Run an experiment to test your hypothesis: Remove Food/Food Group X from your diet for at least a week, maybe two. Carefully track how you feel. Then add it back to your diet to see if there are any changes in how you feel when you're eating it again.
- Make observations: How did the variables hold up to your hypothesis? Did the absence of Food/Food Group X improve your health?
- Draw conclusions: Were you right about your hypothesis? If not, come up with another hypothesis to test. For example, although

you now know Food/Food Group X is not what's negatively impacting you, it might be alcohol consumption or another food/food group.

You may find that you perform many of these steps when you're trying to solve problems in other aspects of your life. That's not surprising seeing as the scientific method of thinking is one of the most powerful tools you can use! Approaching problems with this method will start to shift your life in a positive way.

Thanks to its enormous impact, when we talk about finding your own path, the scientific method of thinking is what's going to get you there. Remember that in your everyday world, you do what you see others doing and hope to get similar results. Frankly, that's a crapshoot. Through the scientific method, however, you learn to figure out what is right for *you* and you alone. You can take different methods you see and figure out what exactly about those methods works for *you*. Approach your issues with a growth mindset and the scientific method of thinking. As you become better at doing so, you'll fine-tune your methods and make them more efficient and overall better.

We see examples of this method in the *Spiderman* movies starring Tobey Maguire and Andrew Garfield. In the first movies of each franchise, we see Peter Parker learning to use his newfound powers, the ones he acquired after being bitten by a radioactive spider. Montage scenes show Peter then learning how to shoot his webs and figure out what his improved body can do. No one shows Peter what to do or how to do it—he's (literally) conducting his own experiments on the fly.

This expansive, experimental way of thinking is especially useful when things in life change. Change is one of life's constants, and having the kind of mindset and methods that enable you to adjust to change is going to keep you on your fitness path. Say you have an after-work fitness routine set that you've been enjoying for years. You have a gym between your office and your home, so it's convenient. You know how to navigate your routines through the gym; you know how to deviate and adjust your plan when some equipment isn't available. Your fitness routine would be easy if everything stayed just like that for the rest of your life. Of course, that's not going to happen—at some point, you're probably going to move or change jobs, and besides, there's no guarantee the gym is going to stay open for the rest of your life.

Change is why you want to practice the growth mindset and the scientific method of thinking. Together, they'll help you find ways to maintain a routine that gives your body and mind what they need. When something in your day-to-day routine changes, it's going to take some time to find ways to fill those gaps, and it's not always going to be an easy fill-in. Your old gym might have had some equipment that your new gym doesn't. Your new gym might be farther away from your home/job than your normal gym was, giving you less time to spend there. Either way, your in-gym routine is going to have to change. If you aren't aware of the journey and how it relates to your own fitness path, these changes may derail any sort of progress or consistency. You'll likely see yourself as a victim of all these changes rather than a hero who's trying to— who's *going to*—overcome them.

Rules of the Road

> *Learning starts by learning the rules verbatim. True understanding happens when you know how and when said rules can be broken.*

As you embark on the testing phase of your journey, it's important to keep a few rules in mind. These rules are meant to keep your mind open so that you can find creative solutions to your challenges:

- Everything works until it doesn't: Currently, thousands of fitness products, programs, tips and hacks guarantee success (i.e., weightlifting protocols, certain foods or supplements, etc.). Assume these things work to some degree, although you may need to apply the concepts in the proper context/be the exact target audience of a product to get the best results. But the take-home point is that if someone is talking about a particular tactic, it probably works to some degree. It's also safe to assume that at some point, things will *stop* working. Our bodies adapt to the way we train them and our lives are dynamic and ever-changing. There are simply too many variables at play to assume that a given method or guideline is going to work for eternity. The question is whether or not you have the tools to figure out what comes next.

- The answer to most health and fitness questions is almost always "it depends": One of the best pieces of advice I read as a new coach was that most novice coaches will assume there's *one* right answer to a problem. In reality, the answer is "it depends." After having been in the trenches for a bunch of years, I recognized the reality of that answer. When I was just starting out as a coach, I would try to give someone a yes-or-no answer if they asked whether or not a method worked, but with experience, I began to realize that the answer depends on who's asking the question. What's their situation like? What's the greater context of their question? Answering "it depends" means you have to dig deeper to find out what your goals are. You also need to see if they match up to the purpose of the proposed method, whether you're proposing it or someone else is.

- Consistency is king: Imagine sharpening a blade on a whetstone. To get the edge of the blade as sharp as possible, you'd use many consistent strokes along the stone. The more consistent the stroke, the keener the edge of the blade. If you were to press really hard and try to force the blade to sharpen itself faster, you'd ruin it; if you don't give the blade enough passes on the stone, it won't be sharp. The same goes for making progress with health and fitness goals—you can't fix all of your physical issues and accomplish all of your goals in one day. Nor can you get rid of all of your mental barriers overnight. Despite this reality, many people want to see their labor bear fruit immediately and they want to see results yesterday, so they push themselves hard for short periods of time. Meanwhile, they don't pay attention balancing their training regimen with their lives outside of the gym. The result? They get worn out or they get fed up because they don't see the results they wanted in a short period of time. Don't make that mistake! Work on being consistent in your efforts day in and day out, week to week, month to month, year to year.

- The path to freedom is through discipline: This rule may seem counterintuitive because the word "discipline" conjures up images of control and rigidity. It seems to be the complete opposite of what someone might think freedom looks like. To understand this concept, refer back to the previous rule of consistency. There's a massive amount of discipline involved in sticking to your routines! And sticking to your routines is what gives you the adaptations that come from good habits. We often think of freedom as being able to do whatever we want whenever we want. And that would be great...except you probably have life responsibilities that don't allow you to do whatever you want whenever you want, at least not all of the time. Exercise and nutrition are much the same. If you maintain discipline and consistency *most* of the time, you can do whatever you want *some* of the time. A good rule of thumb here is the economic principle of 80/20: roughly speaking, 80% of your revenue comes from 20% of your client base. In fitness, this means you want to maintain discipline about 80% of the time. If you're eating 3 meals a day 7 days a week, that's 21 meals per week. Some quick math says 80% of those 21 meals is between 16 and 17 meals. You can be reasonably free about what you eat for the remaining 20% of the time—that's 4 to 5 meals per week—and still see decent results.

- Make understanding your goal: Most goals that people set have to do with numbers or their appearance. Such goals make sense because they're tangible and you can easily see if you're on track. Tangible goals also make it possible to measure your progress, and if you can measure something, you can adjust and make changes when needed, especially when you're in the testing phase. *But* remember this: beyond tangible goals, your one ultimate goal needs to be to have a better understanding. Not just of what you're doing for your health and fitness, but a better understanding of *everything*. Not just your exercise regimen or your nutritional habits. *Everything*. How well do you understand how your mind works and how your body works outside of exercise? How deeply do you understand the world around you? Do you understand how different points of view can add to your ever-growing view of reality? You must always seek to add to the bigger picture. Improving your big-picture view means you'll have a greater knowledge base to draw from when you need to solve a problem in any area of life. Your ability to solve a problem will make you unstoppable in both life and fitness. By making understanding and being curious part of your mindset, you give yourself more resources. Treat this rule like your consistency and discipline depend on it.

Now that you have a set of rules and a method of thinking that will help you throughout your journey, we can get down to the really hard work! I'm not saying all the physical work you're doing to get in shape isn't hard, but if you're only living within and for the sake of the physical world, you're giving yourself an escape from doing the internal work. And the reality is that while doing the physical work is required, doing the *internal* work is what will help you excel and reach the finish line.

CHAPTER 5

FITNESS IS MENTAL AS WELL AS PHYSICAL

———————◆———————

There is an infinite universe within us of untapped potential and it is 100% real and completely accessible to us. All we have to do is have the courage to take long, hard looks inward.

As you travel along your path, the closer you get to any goal, the harder it gets to finish the job. On your journey, a fierce monster or a daunting obstacle will seek to waylay you. And as you get closer to the end, there's going to be a huge challenge you'll need to overcome in order to achieve your goal.

What most people don't expect is that the challenge will be an internal one. On your fitness journey, physical challenges will make you uncomfortable, yes. That's a given. But the real challenge isn't completing physical tasks—it's arranging your mental focus so that you'll want to engage in those tasks regardless of how hard they are. *That's* what makes the hero noble: they walk *towards* the battle, not away from it. The noblest parts of you will want to do the same. Those are the parts of you that want to find out exactly what you're capable of and what kind of mark you can leave on the world. The problem is that the voice of deceit and resistance lies in each one of us. It's the voice that tells us it's far better to *not* try and *not* look like a fool and *not* get hurt. This is the voice that will threaten to keep you from finding your freedom on your fitness journey.

Success on the journey comes despite hearing that voice. As we become better at recognizing it, we can allow it to say whatever it says…and then we can nevertheless execute the actions we need to take. How? Because of the light dimmer switch effect I mentioned a few chapters ago.

Most of the crucial parts of your journey are going to take place inside your mind, so you're going to need tools to help you navigate that particular space. The best tool to start with is the practice of mindfulness. Simply put, mindfulness is nonjudgmental observation of your thoughts and surroundings. Mindfulness will give you the most honest view of yourself and the world around you; it will shine a light on the inner workings of your physical, emotional and mental processes. By being mindful about your physical body, you'll start to understand how it moves and you'll feel how its parts connect and move in unison. Observing your emotional states will give you insight into what you're feeling. These observations will help you determine what you like about your fitness routines as well as help you understand what methods aren't good for you. Having a better view of your mental processes will help you understand your decisions.

Awareness of your mental, emotional and physical states is the key to change. Such an awareness will allow you to see if you're employing a growth mindset instead of a fixed one. Being mindful will also show you if and when you're using your new rules to solve problems.

A lot of people have been doing the same routines for years—they get into a groove and they never question why they do what they do or if they could start to do something different. I'm not talking about just trying a different restaurant next week or trying that exercise you saw the jacked dude at the gym doing. You want to figure out *why* you make the decisions you do. Do you truly need to go to a different restaurant every week? Do you simply prefer variety, or do you need something new every week due to boredom? Does that carry over into the way you work out? Do you feel like you need to do a different set of workouts every week to keep from getting bored? Do you really need to change up your exercises as much as you think?

There's going to be a difference between decision-making in the everyday world and decision-making on your new path. When you're in the everyday world, many of your decisions may be based on fear and comfort because that's what keeps you in a safe place—fear-based decisions mean we can more or less predict the outcome and avoid putting ourselves at physical risk. This reaction is one of the mechanisms our nervous systems uses to keep us alive long enough to procreate. Making decisions based on comfort likewise allows us to feel safe.

Using either fear or comfort as a basis for decision-making isn't bad since then you won't put yourself in harm's way, at least not from a neurological standpoint. You'll feel safe and secure, and there's nothing wrong with that. However, these emotions become detrimental once you receive your wake-up call, because then you'll have a different and unfamiliar purpose. Acting on fear and comfort at *that* point will eventually derail your journey.

Advancing along your fitness path requires becoming familiar with your own fears and anxieties. Setting out to gain your wellness freedom means you must commit to trying something you may fail at. You are going to tread water in unfamiliar territory; you're going to ask yourself to meet different and new challenges. And that's going to scare you. It's going to feel unsafe for your nervous system because you won't know what to expect.

It takes trust to stay committed to your path without knowing how or where the path will end. You'll have to trust yourself enough to know that you'll show up every chance you get. Our earlier example of sharpening a blade also applies to building trust and confidence in yourself.

You must consistently show yourself that you're capable of making different decisions. When it comes to your journey, the only person who can motivate you is *you*. Yes, you can read all the inspirational quotes you want, but you have to decide to *take action*, including during times when you feel scared and don't feel like you're motivated enough to do what's necessary. That's precisely when you become some*one* and some*thing* different than what you were in the everyday world. It's knowing that the best decision for you is to stay in and get a good night's sleep because the quality of tomorrow's training session depends on it. A good training session after a good night's sleep reinforces the positive pattern. You'll get to the point where you'll want to set yourself up for success every day even if success and a good training session aren't guaranteed.

Another way to look at your new mentality is to approach each day like you're living it all over again. The idea is similar to the notion of living each day like it's your last one on Earth, except with a bit of a twist. At this point, you have an idea of what you need to do on a daily basis to take ownership of your health and fitness. When you add the practice of mindfulness to the mix, you'll observe your thoughts and emotions around your daily habits. You'll know what anxious thoughts you have about going to the gym and what causes you stress when you're planning your meals for the day or the week. You'll know that you'll crave certain foods when you're in certain mental states. Understanding yourself in this manner allows you to plan for situations that would otherwise potentially lead you away from your path.

Planning your day like you're living it all over again takes into account things that can go wrong. Say it's leg day. You know it's going to be a hard workout and you're correspondingly anxious. On the "first" go-around of your day, so to speak, you skip your workout because you couldn't get over the anxiety. Then you ask yourself, "If I were to do this day over, how would I make it through leg day?" Maybe then you remember that you get really amped up when you watch the tournament montage from the original *Karate Kid* movie, so you make it a point to view the scene a few times before your workout. Instead of feeling anxious, you feel like you're the best around and *nothing's* going to keep you down! (Sorry, I couldn't help myself...)

Time-loop stories like *Edge of Tomorrow* are great examples of living the same day all over again. In the movie, Tom Cruise's character must complete a mission to save the day, but he doesn't know how to achieve his goal. Fortunately, by chance, he gains the power of starting the mission over again once he dies. Each time he dies and is "reborn," he knows a little bit more about the mission and the pitfalls and can learn from them. The same applies to your day-to-day life—you'll get some things right and some things not so right, but consistently finding ways to improve your daily habits will add up to bigger results in the future.

This phase—the one leading up to the hardest part of your fitness journey—is an internal one. You must understand that the only person you can control is you. No one else is going to do any of the work for you. People will be willing to help if you show up willing to learn, but those people cannot make you actually *do* anything. *You* must decide what's right for you and find ways to take action.

Time to point out one of the rules from our previous chapter: discipline equals freedom. You might think that fitness freedom means doing whatever you want, but discipline is what builds our confidence that we can get back on the horse if we were to skip a few days here and there. We go from thinking that a break is going to lead to a halt in progress (which could make us give up altogether) to knowing that we can successfully resume our fitness journey (which keeps us on the journey).

Knowing deep down that these choices are *ours alone to make* is what awakens the hero within us. Accepting that *we* are responsible for what happens in our lives can inspire us to do great things. The problem is that many of us will suppress this part of ourselves out of fear. After all, we already know who we are and what our life looks like in the everyday world, but we have no clue what's in store once we step outside our comfort zone. And so we err on the side of caution and our inner heroes stay hidden from the world and from ourselves.

As the hero travels along their path, they must face death. But not just the near-certain death meted out by the dragon guarding the treasure—the hero must kill the previous version of themself. And they must do so *before* the final battle takes place. On the surface, it may seem like the hero must become a completely different person, but that's not necessarily what I mean. It's more like the hero needs to remove all the protective armor they've built around themself to keep them safe. We have to do the same thing on our fitness journeys.

Consciously or not, your habits that have kept you safe over the years are affecting your decision-making. If you haven't prioritized your health and fitness up to this point, that's okay. Frankly, that's not surprising—our culture teaches us to strive for achievement more than for being in tune with our own minds and bodies. You'll have to unlearn that tendency and rebalance your priorities in order to take ownership over your health.

This is where your ego starts to come into play. Your ego has an image of yourself that it holds most dear and does not want to deviate from. The ego will see you as someone who's going to do whatever it takes to chase down your society-based goals. I don't mean to say those goals aren't something we should all shoot for, but I *am* saying that a short list of external goals has nothing to do with your health and fitness. At least, not at the moment. And I'm not suggesting changing the list of things you want to prioritize, either. My suggestion is to *link* all of your goals and priorities to your well-being. See yourself as someone who uses their fitness as a springboard to chase down *all* of their goals, someone who uses their high-functioning mind and body to achieve *all* of their dreams. Imagine the best version of yourself showing up for your loved ones!

You must become comfortable with killing off the image of your former self. You must accept the new version of your self that you wish to become. If you don't, you'll always be battling between two versions of your self: what was and what you're trying to become.

But! Killing off the image of your former self is different than saying that the current image of your self is less-than or undeserving of success. Do *not* fall into the trap of thinking you only deserve success on your journey if you're able to transform into your new image. That could not be further from the truth! The truth is that you must accept the old you and simultaneously have the grace to know that the old version of you was the best you could do with what you knew at the time. And now that you know more is possible, you can thank your former self for getting you this far. That version can lay down to rest so that the *new* version of you may rise from the ashes. You are giving birth to your own phoenix.

This idea of grace and acceptance is what makes moving forward on the path so difficult. When we're not where we want to be in life, we can come to see ourselves as inadequate. And it's hard to see ourselves as inadequate and still be okay with ourselves. Why can't we just *be* the best, most-in-tune-with-life versions of ourselves that we want to be? Because we don't know how to. Yet. And that's okay. To grow and move forward, we must accept our current situation even if we aren't quite the fitness hero we want to be. Once we move forward, *that's* when we can begin to think about slaying the dragon that's keeping us from owning our health and fitness.

And slay the dragon we must! In doing so, we learn the lessons we need to learn in order to deal with the unpredictable nature of life. Alongside those lessons, we also learn to handle the inevitable changes that will occur as we undertake our fitness journey.

CHAPTER 6

THE STRUGGLE AND THE PAYOFF

When you finally realize that it's been you holding yourself back this whole time by giving into your fears, it will floor you.

You've now come to the moment of truth. You've learned how to begin owning your health and fitness. You've learned to test out various methods to figure out what fits your lifestyle and needs. You've learned new rules and changed the way you view the whole wellness picture. And you've learned how to address the mental roadblocks that are rooted in your deepest fears.

The next phase is when the hero faces their greatest challenge. The hero has not yet hit rock bottom, but they're about to...and the rest of their journey will depend on how they respond in that moment. The same goes for your fitness journey: you may have had a few ups and downs while figuring out how to find the best methods and practices for yourself, but nothing has ever flat-out made you want to quit. Until now.

Moments when you want to give up can come out of nowhere. These moments usually happen right when you feel like you're reaching your stride and have figured things out. Then *it* happens: you get injured or your job gets too busy or some huge life change upheaves all of your routines and you feel like you have to start all over again. That's when you start to wonder if everything you've gone through has even been worth it. You ask yourself, "Why should I keep trying to delay the inevitable? I'm going to get old and I can't do anything about that. I'm never going to look like Thor, so why keep trying?" This is the inflection point that leads to a downward mental spiral that can snap you straight back into your everyday world. If you aren't careful, you can fall back into your previous thought patterns.

But if you've taken the rules laid out in Chapter 4 to heart, you should feel prepared for this scenario. You should even be anticipating that rock bottom is going to happen because you know that everything works until it doesn't. Your current routine will work until it gets boring and you no longer want to keep doing it. Your current nutrition plan will work until you move to another city and you're scrambling all over creation to get the same ingredients you used to get at *one* local market. Your after-work gym stop that's on the way home from work is great until you buy a house in the complete opposite direction and add another hour to your gym commute.

Situations like these are the reason this book doesn't harp on one specific protocol or method or type of workout. Sure, all of those things are great for you...until they're not. Workouts have no control over when they stop being effective for you and your lifestyle. It is *you*, the user, who must recognize when things aren't working. You must have the patience and attention to figure out how to adjust your routines.

Your ability to exercise will hit a snag due to injury, stress, your schedule or other responsibilities. It is up to *you* to decide to take different actions. You could continue on the same path, sure, but there's no guarantee it'll continue to work in the ways it previously did. *Everything* in life is variable. The results you'll get depend on the balance of your personal variables. When one variable changes, another variable has to shift in order for you to find balance again.

The other rule to remember is that consistency is king. Even though you might not know which variables are balanced at the moment, you have to keep trying to figure it out. That's the only way you'll succeed in the long run. The only way you'll *fail* is if you stop trying. In a lot of ways, this path and this process are quite simple: just make an effort to consistently try to do better. The idea is to always keep your momentum going, even if it's with the smallest of pushes. You're better off doing the absolute bare minimum for a few years than going hard-core for a year and then stopping altogether.

When you hit rock bottom is when you need to fall back on your allies, mentors and even enemies. When you feel lost is the time to go over the lessons you've learned up to this point. It's also the time to start making use of all the information you currently have.

Bruce Lee once said that we must "absorb what is useful and discard what is not." When figuring out your fitness journey, know that this piece of advice forms the backbone of your whole path. Out of the methods and ways of training and eating you've tried up until now, what has worked? What hasn't worked? What used to work but no longer does? You must always assess your routines to make sure you're using the most effective tools for your situation.

With all that said, there's one minor caveat to this rule: most of these methods will take time to work (or not). You must see them out until the end unless it's blatantly, abundantly clear that you don't want to continue. Some programs are designed to work over a specific amount of time, like a 12-week strength program or a 30-day rebalancing diet. If you only do half the work and expect to see great results, you're going to be disappointed.

When you feel the most lost is when your inner hero needs to come out. It's the voice telling you to keep going even though it's going to be hard to get back onto the horse after a big fall. It's the part of you that wants to keep going even though every other part of you says it's time to give up.

Think of every movie you've seen where it looks like the hero is about to lose. Their arch-villain seems to have them down for the count. The hero is writhing in pain and agony and must dig deep to stand again and make one last effort to try to win the day. But no matter how dire the circumstances, since it's a movie, you pretty much know the hero will find a way. You must have the same belief in your own inner hero.

Granted, movies and real life are not the same thing. There's no guarantee that if you dust yourself off and get up, things are going to work out in the end. Still, it's the nature of your inner hero to try and keep trying until you break through. It's the only way to prove to yourself that you can persevere regardless of the obstacles in your way. When you finally find a way to imbue this belief in yourself, you'll discover that it's the true payoff for your own fitness path. And make no mistake, that kind of belief is something only *you* can give yourself.

You may have thought the payoff for your trouble would be to burn calories or lose fat or gain muscle or run a marathon or step onto a stage. That's what keeps us going at first—we see positive results early on and they keep us coming back for more. But once things start to level off and making the same type of progress becomes a chore, we lose momentum.

Through trial and error, you're going to find that results don't always matter. Like we've already talked about, you're going to get some ideas wrong and you're going to try things that don't work for you. If you're keeping our rules in mind, you're also going to find out some things about your mental makeup while you're spending time in the trenches. You'll come away with a payoff that's more than your gains: the knowledge that the *process* is what counts and that *always persevering* is what matters. Even if you fail for a short time, you'll keep trying because you know that sooner or later you're going to find a way to make some headway.

Buddhism talks about the "law of impermanence." Simply put, the idea is that nothing is permanent. A human life is not permanent, nor is anything contained within that life permanent. Likewise, your state of stagnation is not permanent. You *can* figure out a way back to making progress in whatever way you define it. You won't know the way initially or see a direct path, no, but understanding that a roadblock is impermanent can motivate you to look for a way through it. In essence, traveling your path is understanding how to apply the law of impermanence. Apply the law at any point as a reminder to always move forward and try to find a way through to the next phase.

You've gone through the trenches and figured out how to keep going. You've learned to persevere even though you don't fully know the way through. You now have enough confidence in your ability to figure out how to move forward on your path even though that might mean not making any progress for a while. But that's fine, because in the long run, you know that consistently showing up as best you can *will* lead to a breakthrough.

Now you must take what you've learned and bring those insights back into your everyday world. But it won't be the same world you left, nor will you be the same person you were when you left it. You're going to have to learn how to navigate the road back and apply what you've learned. And as you do, you should expect some pushback from your old life.

Reflections for Part 2 of Your Fitness Journey

➤ Have you used the scientific method of thinking to solve a non fitness problem? How?

➤ What rules do you assume apply to your fitness?

➤ Can you imagine a scenario where those rules may not apply?

➤ What aspects of fitness do you enjoy (if any)?

➤ What aspects do you dislike?

➤ What would your perfect fitness routine look and feel like?

➤ What possible roadblocks can you anticipate in your current fitness routine?

➤ Where would you start looking for possible solutions to said roadblocks?

PART 3
MAKING IT WORK FOR LIFE

CHAPTER 7

SIMPLIFY AND CONSOLIDATE

---•---

> *To some degree, what you were no longer matters. What matters now is what you decide you want to become.*

Now you enter the part of your journey that's going to bring you full circle. You've discovered what you needed to know about yourself and learned some important lessons. This is when you must begin to solidify the new version of yourself in a world you had previously left behind. The problem is that you've changed since then. Consequently, you're going to have to take some time to rebalance all of the equations in your life when you return. You're also going to need to learn how to simplify all the knowledge you've gained. After having spent a lot of time in the trenches learning new information, you need to whittle down said information so that you can create a sustainable and durable system for yourself.

Also, because you know you'll constantly face changes, you must create a flexible system of health and fitness and be ready to deal with change when it happens. Having a framework you can base your decisions on is going to be vital when it comes to staying on your lifelong fitness path. If you're familiar with mental models, the idea behind this framework is the same: as you continue along your fitness journey, you'll continually add to your model and tweak it.

Helpful Mental Models

> *"The whole of science is nothing more than a refinement of everyday thinking."*
> – Albert Einstein

Below are four mental models that can help you along your journey. Each one can lead to a different solution to whatever fitness issue you may be facing. With time, you'll learn to use these models to adjust your approach when needed.

First-Principles Thinking

This model coined by Aristotle helps you boil your problems down to their most basic components. It works as follows:

1. Identify the problem as accurately as you can. Say you want to gain muscle mass and you think you're doing everything in your power to do so.
2. Break down the problem into its fundamental elements. In this case, you need to eat enough calories to grow, eat enough protein to build muscle and work hard enough in the gym.

3. Try to change one or more of the fundamentals. For example, start tracking your calories and protein intake if you aren't already. Make sure you're taking your exercise sets close to muscular failure (i.e., you should only have one or two reps left in the tank at the end of your sets).

4. Build a new solution from scratch. Sticking with the same scenario, your new solution now has a trackable component for calories and another for protein. Your workout regimen requires you to work harder in each set.

Second-Order Thinking

Used by author and investor Howard Marks, this model helps you think about what happens next. While first-principle thinking takes you to the most direct solution, second-order thinking asks questions that focus on the consequences of those solutions.

Using our same example, when you decide you must track your calories and protein intake in order to gain muscle mass—and you must also work out with a certain intensity—second-order thinking asks what happens when you make those changes. What would be the consequences if you put more of your limited time toward your health and fitness? Would other parts of your life suffer, or do you know how to compensate for that shift in the use of your time and attention? Second-order thinking also asks if and how those changes would affect your food budget.

By considering consequences and asking what comes next, you make your well-being a top priority—when you can anticipate problems, you start to think of possible solutions, and when you have possible solutions, you're already in front of your problems. Staying ahead of your roadblocks will help keep you on the path because then your progress is harder to derail.

Map Versus Territory

Introduced by Alfred Korzybski, this mental model helps you separate the plan from the execution of it. Think of the map as a well-drawn-out plan. It will work if you follow it to perfection, but navigating through the territory is what it will actually take to execute the plan and achieve your goal in the real world. That doesn't mean the map is always wrong— rather, it acknowledges that there's only so much a plan can account for. This book, for instance, is a map, which isn't the same as viewing the map's territory in person. A map/this book can give you a rough blueprint to success, but it cannot cover the full, rich territory that is your life experience, nor can it account for the unpredictability of life.

In our muscle-gaining example, you can consult many sources to find meal plans designed to help you gain muscle mass. That's the map. But readymade plans rarely take individual personalities into account: they cannot consider your food preferences, allergies, sensitivities and many other factors. When you personalize a plan with such details, *then* the map is depicting your personal territory.

The same goes for any muscle-building workout plan. It can give you all the necessary exercises and set and rep schemes that in theory will help you build muscle, but a readymade plan cannot account for factors like work schedules, nutrition and available equipment. Consider your territory *before* choosing a plan. If you don't, you may find that your plan has some holes in it when you try to apply it to your particular situation.

The Feynman Technique

Richard Feynman was a famous physicist known for breaking down very complex problems into simple terms. On your journey, you'll acquire an impressive amount of knowledge, and it'll be up to you to solidify and simplify that knowledge so that you can access it in any situation. Allowing things to remain too complex can prevent you from using ideas within different contexts, and using ideas within different contexts is what allows you to form valuable new ideas. New ideas are key to finding better solutions to your problems! Essentially, simplifying ideas makes it easier to form new ones. Feynman's method is as follows:

1. Study your topic. In our muscle-building example, you're going to learn all you can about building muscle. You're going to read books and articles and blogs and then reread them. You're going to watch as many videos and seminars as you can and listen to as many podcasts as you can. The idea is to gather as much information as possible.

2. Find someone whom you can teach what you've learned. The idea here is that in order to teach, you need to learn how to explain

things in a simple and relatable manner. When you start to teach someone, you start to organize all the information you have. The person you teach could be a workout partner, a friend looking for some tips, a client or anyone in between. Or you can stand in front of the mirror and pretend to teach yourself. No, seriously. This works way better than you might think.

3. Fill in the gaps that are exposed when you try to teach people concepts. You're going to realize that you're missing pieces of your explanations when trying to explain ideas to others—you'll see where you don't understand the topic well enough to explain it.

4. Stitch all of your information into a concise narrative. Simplifying our muscle-building example could look like the following: you have to consume enough calories to grow, you need to consume enough protein to build muscle and you have to work your muscles close to failure.

Along with the rules laid out in Chapter 4, these mental models will give you a new mindset, one that can give you all the freedom you want in your fitness journey. Remember, freedom does *not* mean you're free from having to take care of your health and fitness! Freedom means you're free to choose *how* you want to pursue your health and fitness path. To embrace this freedom, you must have mental models, rules and guidelines to work with.

This phase of your journey will be marked by having access to such tools; these mental frameworks will give you the confidence you need to figure out any issue you might face. All that's required is your focus, attention and patience.

But the most difficult part about your journey won't always be applying what you've learned—rather, it will be coming to terms with how others react to You 2.0. Friends, family and significant others get used to having you show up in their lives in a certain way, and when you make changes to your decision-making process, that may affect how others see you.

As we change and make healthier decisions, we assume people around us will be happy for us, and that's often exactly what happens. But some people may *not* like that you've changed because they're used to having you in their lives in a certain way. For example, they might rather still have you as their drinking buddy than as the new version of you who drinks a lot less or maybe doesn't drink at all. The version of you who no longer chooses to consume alcohol the way you used to might make them feel like something has been taken from them, namely their favorite drinking buddy who helped them get through their tough weeks.

But no matter how the people around you perceive the new, healthier version of you, it's important to keep making the kind of decisions that have put you firmly on your health and fitness path. Just know that the pull of friends and colleagues wanting you to go back to the way you were can derail your progress and be hard to ignore, especially if you're not yet completely comfortable on your new path. Part of you will want to take shelter in the comfort of your old life. Be ready for this and be ready to combat those thoughts within your mind.

And also get ready to embrace the views of health and fitness you'll have once you solidify your mental models and new rules! In the next chapter, we'll go over what this can ideally look like and what you'll want to shoot for going forward.

CHAPTER 8

NEW FITNESS VIEWS

———————◆———————

You have the power to visualize your future and make it reality. But you must be clear with that image! The more clear and the more detailed your picture is, the easier it is to walk towards it.

Changing ourselves requires us to shift the way we *view* exactly what we wish to change. On a journey, the hero must specifically change the way they view themselves and what they're capable of. They must have a different view of how they can affect the world around them. This phase—the resurrection phase—is when the hero ultimately passes the final test. Your own fitness journey is much the same. But remember that passing your ultimate fitness test isn't so much about achieving a specific goal! Your ultimate test is to come away with a new view of fitness, namely the idea that fitness does *not* need to look a certain way. You do *not* have to do one specific type of workout or stick to one type of meal plan.

In your everyday world, supplement pitches and social media advice can influence you without you even realizing it. That's not to say none of those things are useful—some of those supplements might actually help you and some of that social media advice may come in handy. But what matters is that you've *tested those things out* and you know what's actually useful for you. Now you have a filter that helps you sort out what's relevant to your progress and what's not. You can make do when something random comes up and throws off your current routines.

Remember too that you have to become someone else on this journey and that your path to becoming You 2.0 starts in your mind and with your thoughts. Although the thought of working out may conjure up images of an intense fitness commercial, that might not be what you want working out to look like for you. You also might not look like the athletes in the commercials, which might make you think you're not going to be able to take your health and fitness as seriously as they seem to be taking theirs.

These are understandable reactions to what mainstream media and advertising represent as being "fitness." For most people, fitness isn't going to look like those images, and that's okay. You have to be able to see yourself succeeding in a way that's authentic to you. *But* you must also view yourself differently in that space compared to how you have in the past, back when you saw yourself as a person who couldn't make progress. In short, you're going to have to start imagining a different version of yourself.

If you're thinking about your past failure(s), you'll wind up reliving your past. Instead, you must think about yourself as the future version of you that you want to become. Granted, it might be tough to imagine what it feels like to take complete ownership over your health and fitness, or maybe you don't actually know what feeling good about your health and fitness is supposed to feel like. So let's paint a picture of future you.

When you take ownership over your well-being, you know your body's basic needs. You know you need to strength train your body as well as move it through various ranges of motion. You also need to condition your cardiovascular system. The future version of you has preferred methods and ways of practicing these skills but can also adjust when something comes up—no matter what, You 2.0 can still give your mind and body what you need. You're comfortable with your nutrition and don't fear any type of food or ingredient. You know you need food to fuel your workouts and you're not worried about earning your food.

You 2.0 trusts yourself to make the best decisions about your health and fitness. Yes, you make use of guidance from professional advisors like doctors, therapists and coaches, but you don't wait for them to tell you what to do. While your professional allies help you make the best decisions for yourself, they don't make decisions *for* you—you make decisions together.

You have both long-term and short-term goals. Deep down, you understand how your short-term goals affect your long-term goal of lifelong health and fitness. You understand that consistency is the key to any type of long-term success and are consequently consistent week in and week out, month after month, year after year. You're so consistent that you don't even realize how much freedom you've earned for yourself! Your discipline allows you to take a week or two off for a vacation. You eat whatever you want within reason and then get right back to your routines the second you get back home. You can go out once in a while and have a meal that most would gawk at because you're consistent for the rest of the week.

You're constantly fine-tuning your approach. You're aware of what your body and mind need to maintain optimal function and you're always on the lookout for tools that will give you an edge in function. At the same time, you do *not* jump from one thing to the next haphazardly. You trust your instincts when you come across a method or an exercise you know could be useful, and you also trust yourself when you know something won't be a good fit for you. You're able to carry that trust into any other aspect of your life that affects your well-being. You understand how to integrate anything you find useful and you're fine with ignoring anything that isn't.

Reread those paragraphs again. And again. And again. Read them until you can visualize yourself in *all of those instances*, completely owning your health. Remind yourself of that image over and over again! Eventually, when you're done imagining those situations, you actually *will be* that person. It's a way of transporting yourself from your everyday world into the new world and your new mindset. Even if you don't know exactly how you're going to get there, in your mind, you'll already be living in your new world. And as the saying goes, knowing is in fact half the battle.

CHAPTER 9

THE REAL POWER WITHIN

———————◆———————

All the best thoughts and ideas in the world don't matter in the end if you don't act on them. The freedom to act comes from a trust in yourself and the process.

You've entered the final part of your journey, the part where the hero triumphantly returns home. But you're not the same person you were when you embarked upon this journey—you've grown and discovered a lot about yourself and the world around you. This is the throne room scene at the end of *Star Wars: A New Hope*, when Luke and Han (but not Chewie) are presented with medals. In the fitness world, that medal represents the understanding that you already have everything you need: a working mind and a working body. With those two things, you can bend the world to your will if you understand how.

Remember, the entire process of owning your health needs to come from within. You must decide to take ownership of it and you must decide how you want the future version of you to look and feel. And then you must do your best to embody that new version of you *every day*. That's how you avoid getting sucked back into your old ways after returning from your journey—by consistently paying attention to your thoughts, you maintain your progress.

And *that* is how and where you'll find your freedom. Freedom from the stress and anxiety of having to have everything all figured out. In the everyday world, you paid too much attention to trying to make sure everything was perfect. On your fitness journey, however, you realize that the process is *not* about finding the perfect setup and routines but rather about consistently taking action and trusting that those actions are going to add up to a positive result in the end. You know how to adjust your actions whenever you catch yourself straying, and you're able to stay present while you take action. That way, you can assess on the fly how you need to fine-tune a part (or even all) of your process.

The elixir is your mental framework that sets you up for success. Your belief in your path allows you to focus on both your long-term health goals *and* your short-term goals. You weigh each decision you make and decide whether or not it will be positive for your long-term goals. You're able to determine how important one particular decision may be with respect to your long-term goals. A few extravagant, calorie-heavy meals a month for the rest of your life aren't going to derail your progress, not if you're making decisions meant to keep you lean and building muscle the rest of the time.

If you apply this kind of discernment to most of your choices, you're going to be okay in the long run. The same reasoning goes for your workouts: even if you have a few weeks of lackluster workouts, that's not going to affect your lifelong health and wellness. What *could* be very detrimental would be if those lackluster workouts were to cause self-doubt, because doubt could cause you to fall off the wagon for years, ultimately robbing you of your freedom.

Freedom in a fitness sense is something only *you* can give yourself. By now, you have some type of mental framework you're using to work out your fitness decisions. That means you're allowed to make any decision you want when it comes to your well-being *as long as the decision fits within your framework and aligns with both your short- and long-term goals*. You're free to make decisions outside of those parameters as well, of course, but you do so knowing the possible consequences. You also accept that only *you* are accountable for the consequences of your actions—no one else is. *That* is what it means to take ownership of your decisions: you can make any choice you want as long as you're the one who owns the results and you don't blame anyone else for any unfavorable outcomes.

At this point in your journey, you see the process as a dynamic one. You'll absorb anything that's useful and disregard anything that's not without judging— you no longer need to label anything as "good" or "bad" when it comes to your health and fitness. It simply comes down to the fact that some things serve you and others don't.

That realization doesn't put you above anyone else just because they see the world differently. The job of the mind of a fitness hero is not to judge but rather to attend to their own needs as they see fit and to allow others the space to take their own journey. A fitness hero also assists others along their path if they ask for help because the fully realized fitness hero can serve as a mentor to others. At the same time, though, the hero knows they aren't gatekeepers to knowledge—they're merely travelers along the way just like everyone else.

But fitness heroes also know they have the ability to make things easier for other people. They could likewise make things harder for people if they wanted to, except that fitness heroes know making things harder for others doesn't make things easier for themselves. Far from it—encumbering others only serves to dampen their own power and make themselves smaller. A true hero does not fear the success of others! A true hero wants to see everyone succeed. They don't act based on a zero-sum-assumption fear of lack—they act as if there's enough success to go around the world twice over. And they never doubt that truth.

So now it's *your* time to step up! You've read the map and you know the road you must travel. You don't know exactly what you'll encounter on the road, it's true, but you know you have everything within you to meet and surmount any challenge.

Your mind and your body are your tools for cultivating a life of health and well-being.

You know the way. Surrender to it. Live it. Most of all, embrace it.

You no longer need to run away from your path. *A hero* is who you are meant to be.

Reflections for Part 3 of Your Fitness Journey

➤ How would you apply the mental models presented to your current fitness routines?

➤ Are there parts of your routine that you find complicated? Can any of these models help you simplify those parts?

➤ What are some of your current views of fitness?

➤ How would the future you look at those views differently?

➤ Begin visualizing what the new version of you looks like.

➤ How does it feel to trust yourself to take care of your fitness needs?

➤ What does the rest of your life look like when your health and fitness have improved?

➤ How has the world around you changed now that you've earned your fitness freedom?

CITATIONS

Titanic. Cameron, James, director. Paramount Pictures, 1997.

Harry Potter and the Sorcerer's Stone. Rowling, J.K. New York, Arthur A. Levine Books, 1998.

The Lion, the Witch and the Wardrobe. Lewis, C.S. ZonderKidz, 2005.

Arrow. Developed by Berlanti, Greg, Guggenheim, Marc, and Kreisberg, Andrew. DC Entertainment, 2012– 2020.

Darkwing Duck. Created by Stone, Tad. Walt Disney Television Animation, 1991–1992.

The Hero with a Thousand Faces. Campbell, Joseph. New World Library, 2008.

The Writer's Journey: Mythic Structure for Writers, 3rd ed. Vogler, Christopher. Studio City, CA, Michael Wiese Productions, 2007.

The Lord of the Rings. Tolkien, J. R. R. HarperCollins, 1991.

Lord of the Rings: The Fellowship of the Rings, extended cut. Jackson, Peter, director. New Line Cinema/WingNut Films, 2001.

Iron Man. Favreau, Jon, director. Paramount Pictures, 2008.

Star Wars Episode IV: A New Hope. Lucas, George, director. Twentieth Century Fox, 1977.

The Karate Kid, Avildsen, John G., Conti, Bill, and Brooks, Arthur, directors. Columbia Pictures, 1984.

Major League. Ward, David S., director. Paramount Pictures/20th Century Fox, 1989.

The Lion King. Allers, Roger, and Minkoff, Rob, directors. Buena Vista Pictures, 1994

Mindset. Dweck, Carol S., Ballantine Books, 2008.

Turning Pro, Pressfield, Steven, and Coyne, Shawn. US Baker & Taylor, 2012.

The Matrix. Wachowski, Lana, and Wachowski, Lilly, directors. Warner Bros., 1999.

SPIDER-MAN. Raimi, Sam, et al. USA, 2022.

The Amazing Spider-Man. Webb, Marc, director. Sony Pictures Entertainment, 2012.

Harry Potter and the Deathly Hallows. Rowling, J.K. Arthur A. Levine Books, 2007

Edge of Tomorrow. Liman, Doug, director. Warner Bros., 2014.

The Most Important Thing. Marks, Howard. Columbia University Press 2011

Science and Sanity. An Introduction to Non-Aristotelian Systems and General Semantics. Korzybski, Alfred (1933).

Tao of Jeet Kune Do. Lee, Bruce. Ohara Publications, Inc 1975

"Surely You'Re Joking, Mr. Feynman" : Adventures of a Curious Character. Feynman, Richard P. (Richard Phillips), 1918-1988.. New York :W.W. Norton, 19841985.